The Story

Belle T

Lightho

Built in 1832 and decommissioned in 1902, it has been a tea-shop, a home, partly destroyed during the second world war and lovingly rebuilt in the 50's. Owned and filmed by the BBC, moved due to erosion - and now, Belle Tout has been beautifully renovated and refurbished.

With 360 degree views of the English Channel, Beachy Head, the countryside of the South Downs National Park and the enigmatic Seven Sisters - Belle Tout is unique in every way.

This is the story of the Belle Tout Lighthouse.

by Rob Wassell

RAW
Publications

The Story of the Belle Tout Lighthouse

Published by RAW Publications
www.rawpublications.co.uk

First printed August 2011
Reprinted September 2014

The Story of the Belle Tout Lighthouse
www.belletoutlighthouse.co.uk

International Standard Book Number
ISBN 978-0-9569912-0-1

www.rawpublications.co.uk

Belle Tout's original lantern room
Illustrated London News 5th January 1884 - Inside a lighthouse

The chalk boulder strewn beach at Beachy Head, directly underneath Belle Tout

Coastal Erosion

The chalk cliffs of the Heritage Coastline have been eroding for 10,000 years, since the last ice age. This is what keeps them freshly white.

Pounding waves crash against the base of the cliffs, wind and rain lash and take their toll and in winter ice expands to crack and further weaken the cliff until there is inevitably a fall.

The chalk boulders create a temporary barrier until such time as they are washed away and the cycle begins again.

These are referred to as active and passive periods. The active period can result in a fall of three metres of cliff in one go. The passive period could mean that there is no further cliff fall for years.

Sometimes there are exceptionally large falls, such as the one on the 10th January 1999 when 6 metres fell over a length of 70 metres.

Yet, the average rate of erosion continues to work out at 60 centimetres per year. It is suggested that, as global warming continues and sea levels rise, this rate will increase.

Artists impression of Neolithic enclosures, Neolithic arrow head and Beaker pottery

Origins of Belle Tout

Belle Tout is the name of the elevated promontory upon which the current lighthouse stands and from which its name is taken.

The earliest inhabitants of the area of Belle Tout were from the Middle Neolithic to Middle Bronze Age Era, circa 3500BC to 1400BC, with three distinct earthwork enclosures - now partly lost to erosion. There is also evidence of Beaker settlement. The term 'Beaker' was coined by John Abercromby, a Scottish soldier and archaeologist, due to their distinctively shaped pottery.

Further evidence suggests Late Iron Age or Roman use for grazing between 100BC to 400AD.

It appears that 'Belle Tout' is not French, as some people believe, but more likely in fact to be Celtic. 'Belle' taken from, 'Bael', the 'God of War' and 'Tout' for 'lookout'.

In 3500BC, we can guess that the cliff extended 3.3km out to sea - a sea which itself was only formed around 10,000 years ago when the low-lying tundra that is now the channel was flooded with Ice Age meltwater from the North Sea.

Shipwreck off Beachy Head

Shipwreck off Beachy Head

1706 Parson Darby's Hole

The towering white cliffs at Beachy Head have long been a landmark for mariners. Yet a shelf of saw-like rock threatens danger to any vessel that comes too close to the shore. Having taken its toll of sailors' lives for centuries, Beachy Head remains a danger spot even today.

The government had been petitioned since 1691 to build a lighthouse at the top of the cliff, to provide a much needed warning for nearby ships.

Thomas Offley, Lord of the Manor of Birling, agreed to allow a lighthouse to be built on his land. Yet, despite the request being forwarded to the Corporation of Trinity House, no action was taken. For over a hundred years, ships were still wrecked and sailors continued to lose their lives.

In 1706, Jonathan Darby took up his role as Parson of the Parish of East Dean. He was deeply concerned at the number of drowned sailors, and especially so when an 800-ton schooner ran aground with the loss of all of her crew.

With his very own hands, he dug out a series of tunnels in the cliff with a cave 20 feet above the high water mark.

Two boys beneath Parson Darby's Hole in 1899

Wreck at Beachy Head

Wreck at Beachy Head

It is from this cave that he shone a light which warned of the dangers of these shores.

Some 200 years later, part of the cave still remained. In 1919, The Daily Chronicle reported:

"Just beyond the High-browed Headland of Beachy Head, on the next eminence of Cliff marked by the old, now disused Belle Tout Lighthouse, there is a Cave going deep and deviously into the bosom of chalk known far and around in the district as 'Parson Darby's Cave' or, more shortly, 'Darby's Hole'.

Under the Belle Tout Cliffs, where the rocks stretch far outward to sea, utilising a deep fissure in the chalk, with chisel and axe he hewed out a wide chamber with side recesses for shelter from the wind, and he connected this with the beach by a sloping tunnel and a stair of steps."

Today, there is no remaining sign of Parson Darby's Hole, washed away by the relentless tides, yet his brave actions saved many lives.

Parson Darby died on the 25th October 1726 and his grave in East Dean churchyard reads:

"Here lies the body of Parson Darby. He was the sailors' friend."

The East Indiaman, The Thames

Coonatto, Adelaide, Australia, 1860s

All that now remains of the Coonatto that sank in 1876

1828 The First Lighthouse

When the East Indiaman, The Thames, became grounded and 'stuck fast' on the 3rd February 1822, the petition to erect a lighthouse gathered momentum. The Captain of the Royal Navy and Trinity House agreed to attend to this matter.

John 'Mad Jack' Fuller, MP for Sussex, witnessed the event himself and used his personal influence and some of his own wealth to fund the construction of the lighthouse.

In 1828, organised by Trinity House, a wooden lighthouse was erected at the cliff edge where lighting experiments were carried out.

The lighthouse proved to be a huge success and the number of shipwrecks was greatly reduced.

Parry's, 'The Coast of Sussex', published in 1833, refers to this early lighthouse:

"Further on, to the right, is the lighthouse on a projecting neck of land, capable of being seen at much greater distance by mariners when coming within distance of the shore. It has been erected of late years though seemingly called for long before."

The lighthouse, with lantern in place in the late 1800's

1832 Belle Tout Lighthouse

With the application for a permanent lighthouse approved, work began in 1831 on a design by William Hallett and James Walker.

In 1832, Aberdeen granite was conveyed by ox teams from Maidstone to build the tower and locally quarried limestone used to build the keepers' cottage.

On the 11th October 1834, the light from Belle Tout first shone, casting a beam visible on a clear night a distance of 22 nautical miles.

30 Argand lamps, fuelled by Colza (rape seed oil) revolved on a mechanism which produced light for fifteen seconds every two minutes.

The mechanism worked on a clockwork counterweight which needed to be reset by the keepers every two hours.

Cliff erosion was an increasing concern, both for the effectiveness and the future safety of the lighthouse. In 1893, a heavy fall resulted in the loss of 85,000 tons of chalk. In 1896 an even larger fall reduced the distance of the lighthouse from the edge of the cliff to just 70 feet.

The lighthouse, with lantern removed in the early 1900s

1902 Decommissioned

The cliff top was often obscured by fog and in such conditions the flashing light could not be seen from the sea. Boats and ships sailing off the Eastbourne coast were then as vulnerable as before the days of the lighthouse.

The problem was solved in 1900 when a new light-house was built on the rocks below Beachy Head. The Eastbourne Gazette contained the following article on 16th April 1902:

"A newly issued notice to mariners from Trinity House says that it is intended that on, or about 2nd October next, to exhibit from sunset to sunrise a white flashing light from the new Beachy Head lighthouse and to establish an explosive fog signal there. The light from the present lighthouse at Belle Tout will be discontinued."

The light from Belle Tout flashed for the last time on 27th September 1902. A year later it was decided that it would not be demolished. The Corporation of Trinity House sold the building and gardens to Mr. Davies-Gilbert who ran the premises as a tea house.

Postcard from the early 1900s

Postcard from the early 1900s

A Judges postcard, The Old Belle Toute Lighthouse, Beachy Head, Eastbourne

Enjoying the views in a postcard from 1904 and two further postcards above

Various photos from the 1920's and 30's

1923 A Physicians Home

In 1923, the physician, Sir James Purves-Stewart, saw an advert for a 'lighthouse for sale'. He and his wife drove down that very day and having decided it to be the perfect weekend retreat, bought Belle Tout for £1,500.

Already partially modernised, Purves-Stewart carried out further improvements which included a new 'motor road', a garage, an 'electric plant', terraced lawns and an artesian well, sunk 260 feet deep into the cliff and, finally, an additional storey.

Purves-Stewart recorded his experience at Belle Tout in a book, published in 1939, called 'Sands of Time'. "Its tower is distant about thirty yards from the edge", he stated, and quickly sought advice:

"Soon after taking possession we read a warning article in the local press, stating that owing to coast erosion, grave fears were entertained for the safety of the lighthouse. We decided to secure expert advice. A professor of geology came down from London and, after examining the position, informed us that the coast erosion was undoubtedly going on at a steady rate, and that at the end of six hundred years our tower would find itself at the very edge

The Belle Tout lighthouse, as it appears in Purves-Stewart's book, Sands of Time

Enjoying the delights of Beachy Head

of the cliff. This calmed our apprehension and relieved our insomnia. We still have about five hundred and eighty years to run."

Purves-Stewart also recounts a royal visit in the same book:

"In 1935 King George V and Queen Mary did us the honour of spending an afternoon at the lighthouse, during a time when His Majesty was convalescing in Eastbourne. They were delightful visitors, easy to entertain. My wife conducted Queen Mary all over the house, displaying our modest family treasures. Meanwhile King George entrusted himself to me as a separate guide and took a keen sailor's interest in the various gadgets which had been fitted up. When we came to the foot of the narrow spiral staircase leading up to the lantern tower, Queen Mary was already aloft in the glass dome, enjoying the view. She called down to him: "George, don't come up here. It's far too steep for you", To this His Majesty replied "Dammit, I'm coming." And he did. Later he settled down in our sitting-room in an easy chair and thoroughly enjoyed himself, listening and laughing at funny stories."

Various photos of Belle Tout during and immediately after the war

1939-1945 The War Years

During the Second World War, much of the nearby land was requisitioned by the war office. The lighthouse stood at the edge of an anti-tank range.

Belle Tout was hit many times by Canadian troops, their gunfire causing significant damage. The gunnery report from the 12th February 1943 states: "Belle Toute is scarred to the tune of 18 hits to date. All of them accidental of course."

When Sir James Purves-Stewart, now 78, returned after the war, he was horrified at what had been done to his home. He eventually received war damage compensation of £5,000 which he donated, along with the lighthouse, to Eastbourne Corporation.

Belle Tout lay in ruins. Whilst locals called for it to be demolished, the Corporation proposed that it should be turned into a youth hostel.

In the meantime, the site was sealed off to protect the public from the crumbling remains and the unexploded shells that littered the garden.

Belle Tout was finally saved from demolition when it became a Grade II listed building in 1950.

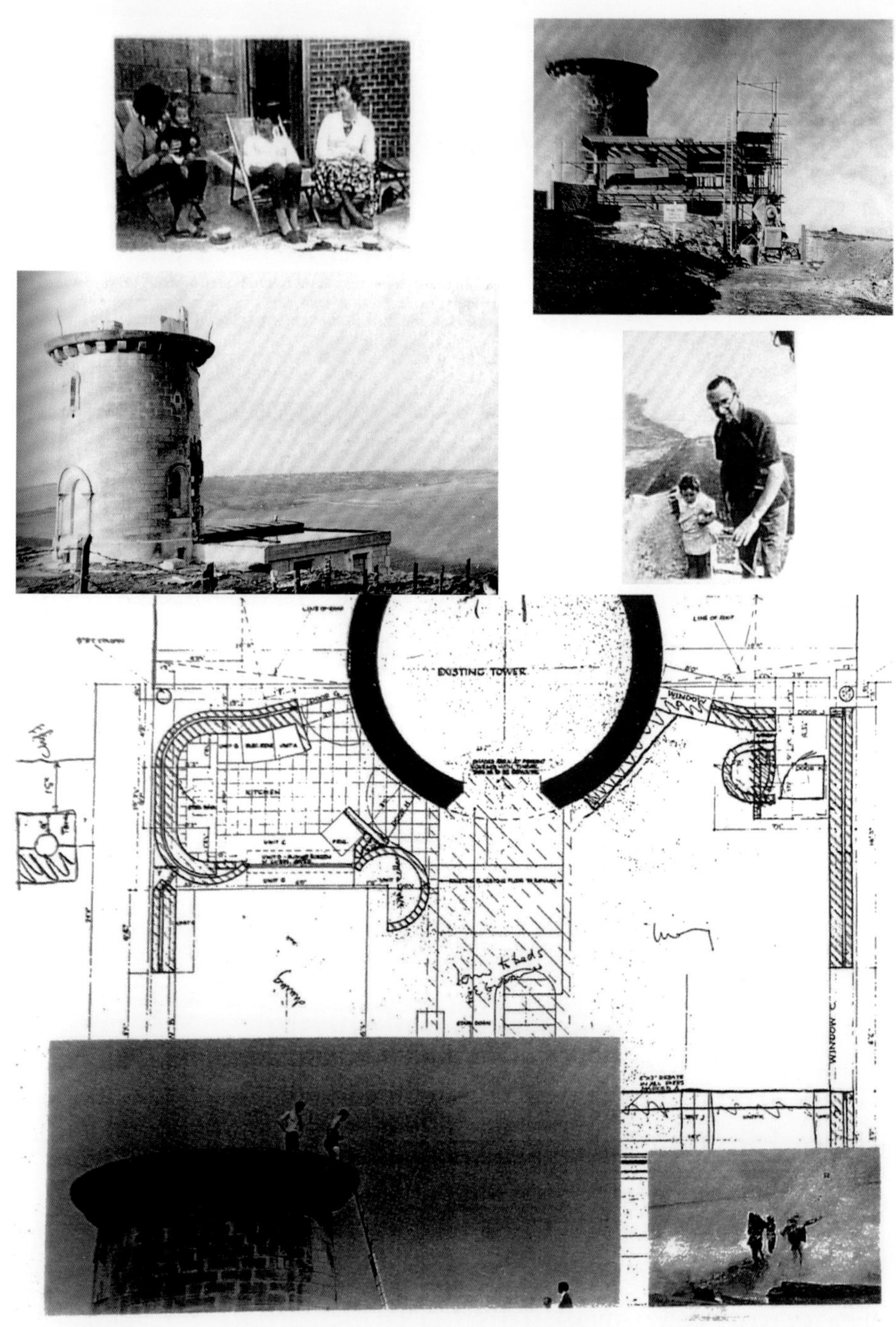

Various photos of the Cullinan family and Belle Tout during the renovation

1955 A Family Home

In 1955, another physician, Dr. Edward Revill Cullinan and his wife, Dorothea Joy, bought a 90-year lease on the disused and ruined building.

It was to be the London couple's idea of a charming country home where he 'took refuge, as often as his busy life allowed'.

With the help of his family, they removed the broken lantern room and restored the tower and the lower ground floor, upon which a new first-storey living area was built. A septic tank, mains electricity and water were also added.

Dr. Cullinan's son, Ted, an aspiring architect, was just 18 when he produced the designs for the new living quarters for the family home.

In 1965 on the 16th March, Dr. Cullinan died at the age of 63.

The British Medical Journal obituary notice from 27th March 1965 states: "He was at his best at the bedside, where the warmth of his personality and his genius for handling patients and their relatives would bring confidence and restore equanimity in the most difficult situations."

Scenes from the BBCs 'The Life and Loves of a She-Devil'. Copyright BBC

1980s An Author and BBC

In 1980, Belle Tout was sold to author, Noel Davidson, who lived at the lighthouse for six years.

In 1986, the BBC considered Belle Tout the perfect location to film their television adaptation of Fay Weldon's 'The Life and Loves of a She-Devil' and purchased it from Mr. Davidson.

The film set was a substantially larger structure, built from timber and glass, surrounding the underlying building with a large cliff-edge balcony. The lantern room was reinstated, the garden landscaped and a swimming pool added.

This was to be the lighthouse 'love nest'.

The award-winning four-part serial starred Patricia Hodge as Mary Fisher, Dennis Waterman as Bobbo and Julie T. Wallace as Ruth, the she-devil. Tom Baker also made an appearance as Father Ferguson.

The BBC subsequently dismantled the film set and sold Belle Tout to Paul and Shirley Foulkes.

The Foulkes' set to work refurbishing the lighthouse and decided to have the lantern room reinstalled for themselves.

BBC set builders at work

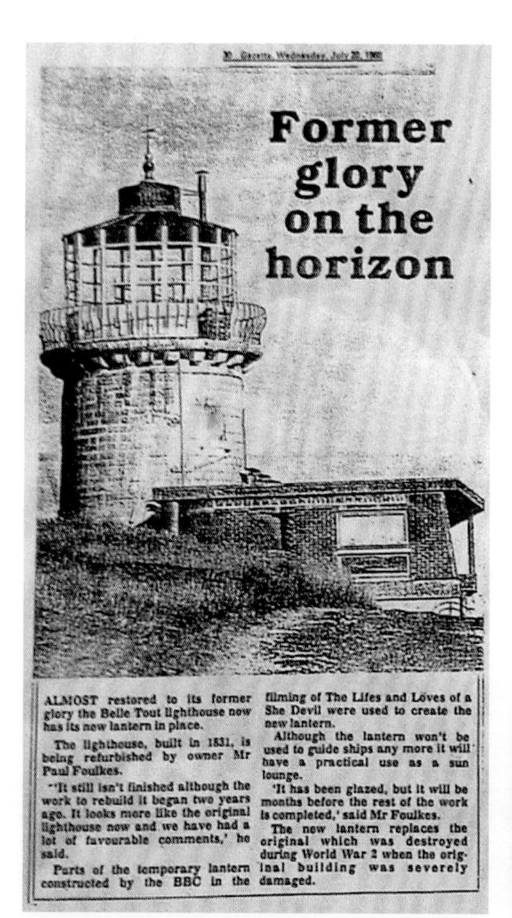

Former glory on the horizon

ALMOST restored to its former glory the Belle Tout lighthouse now has its new lantern in place.

The lighthouse, built in 1831, is being refurbished by owner Mr Paul Foulkes.

"'It still isn't finished although the work to rebuild it began two years ago. It looks more like the original lighthouse now and we have had a lot of favourable comments,' he said.

Parts of the temporary lantern constructed by the BBC in the filming of The Lifes and Loves of a She Devil were used to create the new lantern.

Although the lantern won't be used to guide ships any more it will have a practical use as a sun lounge.

'It has been glazed, but it will be months before the rest of the work is completed,' said Mr Foulkes.

The new lantern replaces the original which was destroyed during World War 2 when the original building was severely damaged.

The Gazette, Wednesday July 20th, 1988

The BBC set and landscaped gardens

New lantern room lowered into place

The Gazette, from Wednesday, 20th July 1988 reports on the story:

"Almost restored to its former glory the Belle Tout lighthouse now has its new lantern in place.

The lighthouse, built in 1831, is being refurbished by owner Mr Paul Foulkes. 'It still isn't finished although the work to rebuild it began two years ago. It looks more like the original lighthouse now and we have had a lot of favourable comments,' he said.

Parts of the temporary lantern constructed by the BBC in the filming of The Life and Loves of a She-Devil were used to create the new lantern. Although the lantern won't be used to guide ships any more, it will have a practical use as a sun lounge.

'It has been glazed, but it will be months before the rest of the work is completed,' said Mr Foulkes.

The new lantern replaces the original which was destroyed during World War 2 when the original building was severely damaged."

Moving the hydraulic jacks into position (The Argus)

The impressive work carried out to move a lighthouse (The Argus)

The Moving of Belle Tout

When the Roberts bought Belle Tout in 1996, they admitted it was because they 'fell in love with it', yet they knew something would need to be done about its close proximity to the edge.

In 1997, working together with Abbey Pynford, they revealed their ambitious plans.

In November 1998 a huge noise 'like thunder' disturbed the Roberts, who quickly fled. They returned when it was safe to find 30-40 feet of cliff in front of Belle Tout had disappeared.

Working around the clock for three months, Abbey Pynford prepared for the move, digging underneath the foundations to build a concrete platform. 22 independently computer-controlled jacks were slid into tunnels, positioned to lift the lighthouse two feet into the air and to slide backwards 56 feet (17 metres) on four greased concrete runners.

The previous owner, Joy Cullinan, pulled the lever at 9:15 on 17th March 1999, but the whole process took a little longer than expected, with Belle Tout finally resting in its new position at lunchtime on Saturday 20th March.

Belle Tout Lighthouse in June 2007, in desperate need of renovation

One Man's Plan for Belle Tout

Rob Wassell has always loved the area of Beachy Head and when, in May 2007, he found out that the lighthouse was up for sale, he had a crazy idea - to try to buy Belle Tout by public subscription and open it to the public.

Talking to visitors at Beachy Head proved that the idea was not so crazy after all - everyone loved it and pledged their support.

The Belle Toute Lighthouse Preservation Trust gained extensive coverage in the papers, on radio and on television.

However, just three days before going on air on the BBC's The One Show in September, someone made an offer for the lighthouse. Rob felt it inappropriate to continue, sat back and waited.

After months of offers falling through and a steady stream of potential buyers, in early January 2008 the Trust had another chance.

An exciting few months brought new opportunities and another planned appearance on The One Show. Then the news emerged that another offer had been put in for the lighthouse. This time it was accepted - Belle Tout had been sold!

Shiraz May 2008

Living Room May 2008

Living Room & Dining Room May 2008

Captain's Cabin May 2008

Living Room February 2009

New England February 2009

Old England February 2009

Outside Old England March 2009

In the Shaws' Safe Hands

In April 2008, Belle Tout was purchased by David and Barbara Shaw.

Closer inspection revealed just how dilapidated Belle Tout really was, from pools of stagnant water underneath floors, to wrapped up clothes wedged into the gaps between the windows.

Their plans were to renovate and restore Belle Tout and let the public stay in this wonderful place. The ambitious schedule to open in eight months was continually delayed and set back.

Completed work had to be undone and re-done to fit new windows. Conservation groups were insistent on specific design features. Delays with the sub-station meant that the lighthouse didn't have enough power. The council were difficult with plans for the all-important access road and the bomb disposal unit dealt with unexploded shells.

It was an increasingly stressful time for the Shaws when nothing was going quite to plan, costs were massively over budget and the council caused a great deal more aggravation.

Yet, together, thankfully, they continued...

Howard - January

David (Archer) - February

John - March

Bez - April

Matt - May

Karl - June

Paul - July

Danny - August

David (Shaw) - September

Simon - October

Hutch - November

Kevin & Erin - December

The Belle Tout Builder Boys charity calendar 2010

A Charity Calendar

In March 2009, Barbara Shaw had a great idea - to produce a calendar in support for Cancer Research's Everyman charity.

The builders were happy to help, some more keen than others to get their 'kit off' for such a good cause.

Rob Wassell did the photography, calendar design and helped with promotion.

Channel 5's 'Build a New Life in the Country' featured the calendar shoot as part of the programme about the restoration of the lighthouse.

In addition, The Collaborative Project produced an online competition called 'Spot the Builder' to find Matt hiding somewhere in the scaffolding. The lucky winner was Lizzy Turner from London.

It was a great deal of fun for a good cause and a notable event in the history of the lighthouse.

'Build a New Life in the Country' was aired in January 2010, updated after the lighthouse opened with extra footage including interviews with guests, and re-shown in July 2010. It is a programme that is frequently repeated and available 'on-line'.

Beach Hut

Old England

Shiraz

Captain's Cabin

New England

Living Room

Keepers' Loft

Dining Room

A Unique Bed and Breakfast

In March 2010, Belle Tout opened its doors, offering themed rooms in a unique building that ensures a comfortable and memorable stay.

David Shaw remarked in Channel 5's 'Build a New Life in the Country', "I bought the lighthouse not with my head but with my heart." Also, he admitted that he probably wouldn't make a return on it in his lifetime and that it was probably a "moment of madness".

It is testament to David and Barbara Shaw's vision and passion that we are privileged to stay at Belle Tout today, and for that, we thank them both...

Visit www.belletout.co.uk to book your stay.

David and Barbara Shaw in the Lantern Room

Rob Wassell, Belle Tout, October 2010

Credits

This journey has been life-changing for me.

The Belle Tout Lighthouse has always held a very special place in my heart. I am honoured to be involved with the lighthouse and often do book signings and talks about Belle Tout and Beachy Head Lighthouses.

I was a key member of the 'Save the Stripes' campaign and have also written a book about the Beachy Head Lighthouse - 'The Story of The Beachy Head Lighthouse' ISBN 978-0-9569912-1-8.

Thank you to David and Barbara Shaw for your support and friendship.

Thank you also to Heather for her love and unending support and Tina for her valuable friendship and eagle-eyed proof-reading skills.

Rob Wassell

rob@belletoutlighthouse.co.uk

Visit www.belletoutlighthouse.co.uk for more information.

All photography, writing and content by Rob Wassell unless otherwise credited.

Many of the old photographs and postcards I have acquired over the years and some of their origins are unknown. My apologies If I have failed to give credit, I have not done so on purpose and will gladly correct this in future if brought to my attention.

Page 6 - Beaker Earthworks by Miles Russell (http://simplyurl.com/P)

Page 21, 23 - Extracts from The Sands of Time by Sir James Purves-Stewart. Sir James died in 1949 and the rights reverted back to his estate 25 years later. I have not been able to find any contact details for his estate, and it has not been for want of trying. I hope I have included this with the estate's blessing as its omission would have left a gaping hole in this publication on the history of the Belle Tout lighthouse.

Page 26, 30, 34 - Thank you to Louise Roberts for being so helpful in providing the Trust with such interesting information on Belle Tout in 2007.

Page 28 - Stills from the 'The Life and Loves of a She-Devil', Copyright BBC and reproduced with their very kind permission.

Page 32 - Photographs of the moving of Belle Tout, courtesy of The Argus.